Reflections

from the

Heart

*A Compilation of Life Lessons &
Poems from the Heart of*

Melvina D. Crawl

Published by Leading Through Living Community LLC

Inquires and orders should be addressed to:
Melvina D. Crawl
Premier Elite Solutions, LLC
info@premiersolutions4u.com

ISBN-13: 978-0692693735
ISBN-10: 0692693734

DEDICATION

I dedicate the poetry section of this book to my mother Doris R. Heath.
I love you mom.

ACKNOWLEDGEMENTS

Wardrobe by Cara Sevier, The Fashion MD

Photography by Joshe Martin

CONTENTS

INTRODUCTION

I reflected upon a few things I would like to share with those who may read this book. My reflections include some snippets from various phases of my life that I hope encourage and uplift you - the reader - regardless of race, ethnicity, gender, sexual orientation, religious background, political party, social class, etcetera. We are all in this "human experience" together, and everyone has a "story" and needs encouragement along life's journey. I am sharing a part of my life in hopes that whoever is reading this book will gain at least one point to make his or her walk in life a little easier and lighten the load with hope.

As we go through this life, not only do we need hope, but we must also have the right resources and tools to get where we are striving to be. I believe personal development is the key to both. Sometimes we do not reach our goals and dreams for fear of failure; but also because we lack the tools and/or support to help us along the way.

Personal development for me has included many hours of reading. I love to read books that help me learn the art of changing my mindset, my beliefs, and the way I implement tasks in order to achieve my desired outcome. In addition to reading, I have also acquired coaching services to help with my business goals. Additionally, I have sought spiritual guidance from my minister to help me navigate through life's issues and understand the word of God, and how God is working in every aspect of my life.

Seeking help is paramount in determining the type of outcomes individuals will have on their journey in life. I know personally the value of admitting the need for help, asking for it, and utilizing it in my life. It is essential one gets the right kind of help, accept it, and apply it in a way that will improve and increase one's growth. It is pointless to seek help if it will not be utilized. Seeking help and not applying it to one's life is like spending money on a doctor's visit and ignoring the advice given to save one's life.

Failing to seek help and apply sound advice can lead to dysfunctional thinking. Dysfunctional thinking can lead you to an early grave. I know: my father, for reasons unknown to me, failed to make lifestyle changes that led to his early demise. Regrettably, he acknowledged and realized the error of his ways too late to do anything about it.

Our decisions about our lifestyles and choices have lasting impact - they can either improve or harm our way of life. Negative choices in life affect us individually, but they also have implications to those closest to us, such as family, friends and co-workers. As such, I am constantly thinking about how my decisions will impact my life as well as my children. I consistently review my commitment to better health, finances, social encounters and spiritual relationship with God. I have often said privately and publically, "I am not perfect. I am not where I used to be, but I am still not where I want to be." Sometimes I fall, sometimes I do not make the best choices in life, but I have come to realize that God is ever so gracious to give us enough chances to get it right.

The older I get, the more I understand Romans 3:23, "For all have sinned and come short of the glory of God." I strive to live a life pleasing to Him and it bothers me greatly when I do things contrary to the will of God, even in my thoughts. What I have learned about myself in the past five years is that I need God more and more. I have to rely on His omnipresence to protect me from unseen and unsuspecting dangers - some due to my naïve thought processes and actions - and particularly when I am most vulnerable.

I was able to admit my vulnerability through self-reflection, looking at myself with an honest eye. To have an honest eye, you have to be willing to peel away the layers to get to the core of your very being. When I read the word of God, I further understand what it means to have an "honest eye." God's word will reveal every secret thought, behavior, motive and detractor in your life. Once these things are revealed, it is up to you to decide to make a change.

Reflections

THE POWER OF THE MIND

I have learned that the mind encompasses some of the most powerful aspects of human life. The mind houses our thoughts, beliefs, intuitions, desires, emotions, intellect, and our capacity to love and hate. It is truly the core of our very being, next to the existence of our souls. So it is imperative that we feed the mind a healthy mental nutritional diet, just as we focus on feeding the physical body edible nutritional content.

Proper nutrition for the mind is in the form of what we absorb through our daily interactions with others, what we listen to, what we read, and what we are exposed to just simply by living. Just like the physical aspects of improper nutrition can have negative effects on our physical body, similarly, experiences of negative nutrition for our minds can result in toxic decisions.

One of the most profound areas in which the above may be witnessed is that of the development of a child. Parents are the first exposure to a child's mind, particularly the mother. From the time of conception, the development of the fetus to being birth into the world, the mind is being influenced. I hope that in the next few segments that your mind becomes filled with encouragement as I reflect upon various phases of my life. One major key to changing your life is changing your mindset. To change your mindset, the mind must receive proper nutrition to strengthen the physical, mental, intellectual and spiritual areas of life.

MOTHERHOOD

It was a cold, wintery, cloudy day on January 15, 2001 when I remember thinking, "Is this the time?" I was nine months pregnant with my first child, anxiously anticipating his arrival. The contractions started coming slowly and then faster, feeling as if muscles were squeezing and compressing; as if a vice grip was being tightened and released inside the walls of my belly. My first labor experience of bringing a child into this world with my husband right beside me was a long, laborious, painful, stressful, yet joyful event. Although it was very long awaited, in January 2001, after a day and half of labor, my first born arrived!!! That day was the day I said, "Welcome to Motherhood!"

Motherhood is a very special assignment that God has given to women. This assignment is not always given due to birth; sometimes it is given through circumstance. However, it does not matter whether you have children of your own or are raising someone else's children; if you are providing care for a child, it is a blessing.

Christopher was my first child, and although his birth process was a challenge, it certainly did not change my desire for more children. When Christopher was about ten months old, I found out I was pregnant with our second child. In January 2002, five days before Christopher's first birthday, I had a miscarriage which was a very painful ordeal, physically as well as emotionally. Life was given and life was taken away.

Four years later, I once again was pregnant, and this time it was a precious baby girl. Christina was born the weekend hurricane Katrina hit the gulf coast. I remember the nurses rotating and leaving out to go fill up their cars with gas. I was concerned about the power going out in the hospital, but the staff assured me the generators would kick in should something happen. As the evening progressed, so did my labor. Finally, the head came out but then everything stopped. Christina was stuck in the birth canal. I remember the nurse getting on top of me, sitting on my stomach to help try to push her on down. I remember the doctor saying it was too late to do a C-section and then announced that Christina's face was turning red and he had to do something. He reached inside me (I could feel his arm pressing against my spine) and pulled my baby's arm out. After he pulled one of her arms out, I had to push to get the rest of her body out. At that point in my life, it was the most traumatic experience I had ever gone through.

We later found out why Christina got stuck: her shoulders measured fourteen centimeters in width! I thank God that we only had to worry about her having shoulder distortion and nothing else major was wrong with her. She was the prettiest, juiciest bundle of joy! I always call her my Angel baby, truly a blessing from God. After having a miscarriage in 2002, it left me with a void in my life and Christina filled it with joy. But I'll be honest: I often wonder, especially on January 11th, the anniversary of the miscarriage, what my second child would have been like... And then my Angel baby brings me back to the present and the joyfulness of being a mother.

Christina was such a sweet baby. She never cried at night and I remember often getting up to peep in her crib, and lay my hand on her back just to feel her breathe. She slept all night, every night. God knew I needed that peace in my life. My husband and I prayed for a daughter, and God gave us the sweetest, juiciest little bundle of joy a couple could ask for! Christina truly is my angel baby. She still goes to sleep easily and sleeps all night.

Around the time Christina turned one year old, we found out I was pregnant with my fourth child. My last little princess came into the world in the Spring of April 2007. I remember a long, painful day of laboring; it was an agonizing experience. The miracle of birth is so amazing that even in the moments of pain and suffering, you still realize the life - the new life - God has given is such a blessing. I treasure all three of the lives that God has blessed me with. Crystal's birthing experience was definitely the most challenging of the three. I will share a few glimpses of that day.

There I lay, laboring in the big open room with my husband standing next to the bed. I had a bad gut feeling and kept telling the nurses that something was not right. I felt very tired and weak. I remember wishing that I could just get this over, but it was very wishful thinking. God said women would endure pain during childbirth and He meant just that. Even with the epidural I felt this undying pain. At one moment, I screamed so loudly that my mother heard me in the waiting room - which was down the hall and through a set of double doors. She came running and burst into the room. I was crying and told her to take my kids home because I did not want them to see me in that state.

My joyous childbirth of my third child had turned into a nightmare. I asked for my doctor to come back in the room. He leaned towards me and I pulled him gently by the collar closer to me and I whispered to him, "Something is wrong….I'm gonna die….I'm gonna diiieee!"

I guess the look in my eyes and the tone of my voice threw him into action mode. He brought in the ultrasound machine and it revealed that my baby was breached - face up, feet first, and very large. The doctor immediately rolled me in for a C-section and my little ten pound bundle of joy Crystal entered this world with a strong set of lungs!

Crystal is such a sweet, smart and loving child. She has the personality that you fall in love with and has a heart of gold! She is always giving, kind and thoughtful of others.

After three births and one loss, I do not foresee writing another episode of a child birthing experience. Four times is enough to last a lifetime. But God only knows what my future holds and if that includes me giving birth, I hope it comes with at least two nannies, a maid, a butler and one stellar… husband!

THE EYES OF A CHILD

Firecrackers popped! Yellow, green, pink, blue and silver sparkles flew across the skies on the late night, early July 4th morning as I entered into this world. Born to the proud parents of Doris Ragin Heath and Clarence Melvin Heath, was a beautiful, pretty brown-eyed bundle of joy - that is how I describe my birth experience!

As I reflect upon my life, I think of my mother with her many skills and talents such as sewing, cooking, crafting, and grant writing; and I realize that I could go on and on forever about my mother's exceptional capacity for greatness. She made so many sacrifices in her life for our family. She was not a selfish mother, in that she gave to so many other children: helping to complete college applications, financial aid forms, making dresses for weddings, and helping make other special occasions grand. No matter what she was personally going through, I never, ever - not one time - saw her give up on helping others. To this day, she is still a friend to all and fierce advocate for the education of all children.

During my life I have encountered so many influential women and men, from the kindergarten assistant, my grandmother, my grandfather, mother-in-law, former teachers, men and women in the church and so many others that I cannot name. I feel so blessed to have had these wonderful examples of strength, endurance and love. It makes me realize how vital it is for young girls and boys to see adult men and women in positive roles early in life.

My grandmother, Rebecca Clark Heath, was such an inspiration to me. She taught me how to think, how to care for others, how to sew, how to cook, how to clean, and about life in general. She would answer any question on any topic I wanted to discuss. I always remember her saying "… keep yourself up"; "hold your shoulders back"; "keep a little rouge on your cheeks" and "wear a little lipstick." She was a very refined woman, loved the finer things in life, and always preferred top quality. I believe this is where I get my desire for wanting the best. My father's father, Marion David Heath, was also very influential. He was well educated, a former school principal, and he always talked about the importance of education. I remember him saying, "You need to get your education." My mother's father, Duncan Ragin, was very quiet and we loved to sit on the porch with him. He was also very talented in laying bricks and he could build anything! He was quiet, but he would answer any question you asked. He was always pleasant, and I remember him always smiling as he watched us play.

Interestingly, both of my grandmothers were master seamstresses. I do not remember my mother's mother, Emma Lee Hamilton Ragin. She lost her battle with breast cancer when I was around one year old. However, my aunts told me many times my Grandmother Emma Lee was a master seamstress and could make anything you wanted - all you had to do was bring her a picture and she would bring it to life! Her talent and skill were passed down to my mother and my aunt Irene, and they are both master seamstresses as well. It is amazing how talents are passed along through generations as long as they are continued to be practiced. I remember learning to sew at an early age, and my parents bought me a sewing machine one Christmas when I was about seven years old. (By the way, my dad was skilled on the sewing machine as well. He would make hats, scarves and one time, he made a suit.)

With my first sewing machine, I remember making a Raggedy Ann doll. Later, I advanced to making doll clothes for my baby dolls. I would make doll clothes by cutting out patterns from brown paper bags. I learned this from watching my mother. She would have me assist her by cutting out patterns and pinning the patterns to the fabric. By the time I was nine, I could sew clothing pieces independently on my mother's sewing machine. One year, I made a pretty green floral skirt and top, and won first place at county and district project achievement through the 4-H program.

Today, I have two daughters and one of them said to me, "I need to take my dress to granny so she can fix it." I said to my daughter, "I know how to sew." She looked at me in awe as if she could not believe what I was saying. I realized in that moment I had not passed along a beautiful talent and skill that brought much joy to my life as I interacted with my mother and grandmother on numerous sewing projects. I failed to pass along not only a skill my daughters needed, but also an opportunity for bonding and shared experiences.

I went out and bought another sewing machine, and now I am teaching my daughters this skill. Today, we do not have the same need for sewing and making clothes that once existed; however, that does not negate the responsibility to prepare our children to be self-sufficient - which includes being able to mend clothing pieces when necessary. Additionally, because so few people sew these days, it is a money making business if you can even simply hem pants or take in a garment.

Not only is sewing a talent, but so is cooking wholesome, good food. Both of my parents could whip up the best meals in the kitchen. My dad really could "throw down in the kitchen." I loved when he cooked T-bone steaks! He always referred to himself as "the Master Chef." I guess between my dad and mom, I am a natural when it comes to cooking. I love it and I love serving food with a rainbow of colors!

I believe when you cook it should smell good, look good and taste good! The aroma of a home-cooked meal permeating the house is one of my greatest joys as a mother. Now I am not implying that there is something wrong with eating out, as I certainly do my share of that! However, I do enjoy cooking for my family. All of my children are learning how to go in the kitchen and prepare family meals. Cooking for me is a past time and it helps me to think, and process information, and clear my mind from the stresses of the world. As a mother, it gives me great joy when I cook a meal and see the reaction my children have, especially when I introduce a new food. I encourage my children to use a rating system to inform me how they enjoy the meals. They created this system for our family. Thumbs up means it is alright, side thumb means so-so, thumbs down means try again or not at all. If it really tastes good, I get a pistol signal; and if it tastes super good, I get a double pistol signal.

I am pretty traditional about sitting at the table and eating as a family. We eat together every day and it helps strengthen the bond between me and my children.

A WIFE

Romans 8: 31-37, *"What then shall we say to these things? If God is for us, who can be against us? He who did not spare His own Son, but delivered Him up for us all, how shall He not with Him also freely give us all things? Who shall bring a charge against God's elect? It is God who justifies. Who is he who condemns? It is Christ who died, and furthermore is also risen, who is even at the right hand of God, who also makes intercession for us. Who shall separate us from the love of Christ? Shall tribulation, or distress, or persecution, or famine, or nakedness, or peril, or sword? As it is written: 'For Your sake we are killed all day long; we are accounted as sheep for the slaughter." Yet in all these things we are more than conquerors through Him who loved us."* This is the scripture my husband and I shared during our wedding vows.

Very kind, loving, gentle, respectful, honorable, and easy to get along with most of the time is how I would describe my ex-husband. No matter what happened between us, he is the father of my three children and for that I am grateful. It started out being a marriage that I loved. We did all the things that strong couples should do to build and maintain a foundation for a long lasting marriage. During our marriage, our faith was challenged by several obstacles including finances, children, job changes and the usual things couples experience. Deep in our hearts there was something else brewing. It was the unspoken words of disappointment, discontentment and simply cold-hearted distance from one another. Eventually, living together was just that…living together. After the third child, things really begin to heat up. Arguments grew and finances got worse with the economy entering a depression, even though it was never truly acknowledged as a depression. In the midst of this, after my baby girl turned one, I went back to work fulltime and our finances recovered; however, our relationship did not. As the next few years passed by, we moved to a new location and started our lives together in a little place that I have grown to love. During this time, my husband got a job promotion in which he asked me my opinion about. Although I said I supported his decision, I really did not like it: it was going to cause us to be separated, we would not see each other, and he would not spend significant quality time with the children.

My husband accepted the promotion, and while our income increased yet again, the marriage began to decrease in quality time, companionship, comfort and care for one another. Any extra time became a focus of family time and doing things with the children, but rarely with each other.

Husband and wife quality time beyond the bedroom walls is so important. Protect it, value it, and make it purposeful. As the deterioration increased, communication on subjects other than our children, church and bills was basically non-existent. Feelings of loneliness, despair and emotional turmoil began to build within both of us. I had been praying about the matter for a while. We received marriage counseling multiple times; however, when a person is absent emotionally and mentally detached from you, coupled with physical separation, it is simply a recipe for disaster.

This book is not about marriage or relationships, but I will say that if you love your spouse, do what is necessary to please God and be honest about who you are, and always first to yourself. Work on you in order to become whole. Then and only then can you be in a healthy relationship with someone else.

Eventually, the emptiness and loneliness turned in to seeking outside sources of being complete and whole. For me, it was throwing myself into business endeavors in the evenings and on weekends when my husband was away. For him, it was a consoling female co-worker that eventually became an affair that led to the ultimate end of our marriage. Many details I respectfully choose not to share at this time, but it was an ugly departure. I remember being told, "I don't love you anymore." A year after hearing those words, I found me and my kids alone in a big two story house without the income to take care of everything that had to be done. I restructured everything by cutting out every unnecessary expense, such as cable television, gym memberships, lawn care service, nail and hair salons, and body massages. I even put the house on the market, but it did not sale. I unplugged electrical appliances from all wall outlets that were not required; eliminated all extracurricular activities; merged any accounts I could and talked to all creditors and made alternative payment arrangements. I consulted with a certified public accountant to help me organize my finances and get ideas about how to manage the household on one income.

In the fall of 2012, I found myself being a single parent not yet divorced. After a month and half of not hearing from my spouse, one Sunday evening after church my daughter asked, "Is my daddy dead?" After hearing her sweet innocent voice, I could stand it no longer: warm, soft, tears began to roll down my cheeks and I could not hold back the quiet pain any more. I managed to say to her, "No he's not dead." There is absolutely no greater pain than experiencing the death of someone who is alive, breathing, and living and yet there is no burial. There is no funeral, there is no moment of visitation. There is no memorial, no burial site and no consolation from others. Our lives felt very empty for months after my ex-husband left: a death had occurred but there was no way to grieve.

My children suffered the greatest, more than I can share or ever express in the words on this paper. I cannot disclose the details of what happened with my children, but I will say that if couples choose not to be together for whatever reason, it is best to keep the children out of the fray yet into hearts of all involved. Talk with the children and inform them of what is going on, and always keep the lines of communication honest and open.

After another year of hoping for reconciliation, we both agreed to end marriage. A year after ending the marriage, my existing job at the time ended and I was in a position yet again of a significant loss of income. I was not worried however, because I knew God was not going to abandon me. I received a new job, although less in pay, it proved to be a very rewarding experience. I am sure I was not the perfect wife, but I do know that whatever happened between us has made me a much stronger and wiser person. My ex-husband is a good person who made some bad choices and so did I. I love him and have forgiven him, and most importantly, I have forgiven myself. In the end, we both will be held accountable for what we choose to do and how we care for our three children God blessed us with during our marriage. God is the final judge. I am thankful, blessed and have a peace in my heart that I know only comes from God. I have been released and I am so truly grateful.

RELATIONSHIP WITH GOD

I remember lying in the bed one night, body stiff and feeling paralyzed as if I could not move. I kept repeating over and over in my mind, "Hold me Lord and don't let me go". I just lay in the bed talking to God, asking for direction for my life and for my children. Reading my Bible had new meaning. I was constantly searching for answers for every decision that had to be made in my life. I discovered so much about myself after looking through a new set of lenses brought on by my new reality. As I studied God's word, I could see so much of my own unrighteousness, and so many areas in which I needed to work to be complete and whole again.

Being single again has revealed weaknesses that I did not know existed. I realize that I am strong in some areas and weak in other areas. My prayer is that God will grant me the time and wisdom to do what is necessary to be pleasing to Him first.

LETTING GO AND MOVING ON

Peace of mind is priceless, and there is no greater treasure than to live in this world and have peace of mind. When God lifts you up and places you on solid ground, it is the best feeling in the world - and it comes from Him and only Him. Jesus made the ultimate sacrifice in giving his life for our sins, and there is nothing that I can do to earn God's unmerited favor. I am so thankful and truly blessed that He allows me to be able to have reconciliation with Him through the forgiveness of sin. I forgive myself, I forgive my ex-husband and that is the only way I can heal. I cannot erase any part of my past or snap my fingers to restore anything that was lost, but I can move forward and leave those things behind.

I am learning so much about myself: my strengths, weaknesses, passions, true loves and most importantly, my desire to do the will of God. I am certainly not perfect and fall short of God's glory, but I get up and strive to be better and do better than I did the day before.

Philippians 3:12, *"Not that I have already attained, or am already perfected; but I press on, that I may lay hold of that for which Christ Jesus has also laid hold of me. Brethren, I do not count myself to have apprehended; but one thing I do, forgetting those things which are behind and reaching forward to those things which are ahead, I press toward the goal for the prize of the upward call of God in Christ Jesus."*

I never thought that after nearly sixteen years of marriage, I would find myself abandoned and divorced with three children to raise. At first, I wondered how I was going to make it financially, emotionally, and physically. I just did not sign up to be a single parent. I grew up in a two parent home and that is all I knew. My life was not perfect as a child and neither were my parents, but I thought that I would have my husband to help with this child rearing business.

The lessons I learned from both my mother and father became so much more relevant when I became a single mother of three. My father always talked to us and said, "Life is about survival and you have to be able to survive in this world." Those words have resonated with me so many times in my adult life. My faith in God became so much stronger during my family crisis. I remember growing up as a child and when things were not right in our household, my mother was always sticking with God. I learned that lesson well, and today I choose to stick with God. I learned enough to know that the devil has plans to destroy us.

Since I am now single again, I have learned to do things differently in my house. I teach my children a level of responsibility that I think they would not have if I were still married. I, too, have learned so much about motherhood in my new role as a single parent. People often say to me, "I don't see how you do it" or "You're doing such a great job." I thank God for life, health and strength because that is how I do it. I especially thank God for my mother who has been there for me throughout everything I have experienced. My mother and my church family have been the main sources of my support.

As individuals dealing with crises we, need support systems to help us through life. People who do not have support systems in place are usually the ones who struggle the most during crisis. No matter how good you are, as long as you are living in this world, expect to have a crisis every now and then. My joys and sorrows of being a wife and mother have taught me that there are moments when it is perfectly okay not to be a "superwoman" and admit, "I need help!" Acknowledgement of "I need help" is a sign of humility, completeness and self-actualization because God did not design us to do it alone.

PARENTAL ENCOURAGEMENT

There are two special moments that I will share about my father's encouraging words. In January 2014, my father departed this world, leaving behind the pain and suffering he endured. I was blessed to have him in my life and my children's lives.

During my childhood, I was often teased about being adopted. My siblings would tease me and even some adults. A few of these adults said to me on more than one occasion, "Where did your parents get you from?" This happened throughout my childhood and into young adulthood. Growing up, I heard it so often that I would go in the bathroom and take my mother's picture and compare my features to her photo to see if I looked like her. One day I said to myself, "She is light skinned and I am dark skinned. She has long silky hair and I have short soft hair. She has deep dark eyes and I have glassy brown eyes. She is thin with small bones and I am thick with medium bones." And on it went... After going through this ritual several more times, I determined that I would find out if I was really adopted.

One day while we were in Chicago, I went to my dad and I asked him, "Daddy was I adopted?" I was thirteen at the time, and this was the first time I had said anything like that to him. At first, my dad just looked at me and then I guess he saw the seriousness in my face. He grabbed my arm and put it next to his arm and he said to me, "You have brown skin like me, you have brown eyes like me, you are smart like me and you know you are just a chip off the old block." Then he laughed and said, "Besides I was there when you were born! You weren't adopted! You belong to me and your mother!" He gave me a hug and told me that he loved me. At that moment, I felt whole and I felt complete. I remember feeling like my daddy saved me! All the doubting from the painful teasing from my brothers and sisters year after year after year vanished instantly. No more doubting and wondering if I was adopted.

The year my dad died, I had been divorced for about five months. During that time, my dad had some very harsh feelings towards my ex-husband, specifically stemming from the state in which he had left me and my three children. During one of our conversations, we talked about my life and he was giving me a daddy's pep talk. During the conversation he shared that, "Me and your mother didn't invest in you to have someone walk all over you". He said to me, "You are smart and beautiful, and you deserve to be treated like royalty." At that moment once again I felt like my daddy saved me. I was in a dark place and he rescued me. He said other things during this conversation that I will always cherish in my heart for the rest of my days. Those last few words of that exchange lifted me to a level of confidence that I hope to always maintain. My daddy left this world instilling in his daughter his love, care and expectations for only the best. I have yet to experience what he meant by "royalty," but I'm sure it did not only mean financial comfort. I just tell myself that when the right man appears I will know because my daddy already told me what to expect.

FINAL REFLECTIONS

When I think of my own mother and I reflect on the lessons I learned from her, such as how to carry myself around boys and men, how to dress and take care of my body, and how to stay faithful to the Lord; I know am truly blessed. My mother was always the rock of the family and she shielded us with her strict rules, which seemed unbearable at times, but now I know she protected us. Those strike rules inspired discipline and high standards in us that yielded success and good relationships with others.

I am so thankful for having the mother God gave to me. I hear of so many children who have mothers that have abandoned them or treated them in inhumane ways that I could never imagine. I have yet to understand, and it will always be a mystery to me, how a woman can be cruel and harsh to her own flesh and blood... and it happens more times than I care to think about.

I pray that as you read these poems in the upcoming

section that you will reflect upon your life. Everybody has a story. As long as you live, life is going to have some battles or giants to face. Be encouraged. Surround yourself with positive people. Strengthen your support system and no matter what, keep moving forward. Be a positive influence on someone else because you never know what they might be going through.

Enjoy the reading.

Poems

A Mother of Noble Character

A mother of noble character
Oh, who can find
She is a friend to talk to
She has an ear to listen
Just so you can have peace of mind

A mother of noble character
Is far more precious than rubies
And far more valuable than gold
Beautiful in the world's eyes
God's grace she beholds

A mother of noble character
Provides wisdom and instruction
For her child
Love and understanding for her husband
She gives unselfishly with a smile

A mother of noble character
Is shaped by God's hand
He placed this special kind of mother
All over His land

A mother of noble character
Makes her home a special, dwelling place
She teaches about God's Love
She's a living example of his grace

A mother of noble character
Doesn't walk around spreading gossip and news
She has enough to worry about and
Not someone else's blues

A mother of noble character
Is an example for all to see
She is the Christian wife
The Christian mother
God intended her to be

A mother of noble character
Praise her while she's here
Love her while she's near

Because of the women in the world
A mother of noble character
Is most precious and most dear

A Mother's Love

A mother's love is a special kind of thing
She has a special kind of joy and happiness
That only a mother can bring

She is very determined to give her children the best
Giving of her time and energy
Even when she needs rest

Her love does not stop at home
But it spreads all around
She just gives, gives, and gives
Sometimes I wonder where all that love is found

I know God knew what he was doing
When he created a woman to be a mother
Only a mother can give
Undying love like no other

No matter how bad a person can be
How troublesome, untamed and wild
She still manages to say
I am here to help you because you are my child

When you need a place to stay
When you need food to eat
You can always call on momma
Her love you just can't beat

Even when she is tired and sick
She still thinks of you
Trying to make sure
She has done all that she can do

I'll tell you - a mother is special in every way
She had to be sent from heaven above
I haven't found a person yet
That can match a mother's Love

A mother's love is a special kind of thing
She has a special kind of love
That only a mother can bring

A Mother's Love

She's My Momma and I Am Proud

Maybe she's no queen
But she's beautiful in my book
She's a very special lady
She's my momma and I am proud

She may not wear fancy clothes
But they're her clothes and they're clean
So what if they didn't come from some
Find department store
She's my momma and I am proud

She may not be well educated
Drive a luxury car or two
She may not live in a big fine house
With a white picket fence
But that's okay
She's my momma and I'm proud

She may not be everything you want her to be
But she is everything to me
No matter what others may think
She's my momma and I am proud

So when you see her walking
Down the street
Head tipped up-not bowed
Just know, she's a very special lady and
I'm proud

She's my momma and I am proud!

God's Gift to the World

Mothers, grandmothers, stepmothers,
In-law mothers, surrogate mothers,
Adopted mothers, surprised mothers,
Any kind of mother
God gave them all

Be thankful for the one you have
And love her for what she is to you

Mothers - God's Gift to the Word

Who's Child

As we trudge along life's way
Some people we meet, we wonder, and say
Whose child is that
Whose child could that be
Pants bust'n slack - He's really puzzling me

Other people we meet, we are very glad to see
I wonder whose child
Walking proud as can be
Walking tall, speaking with much respect
Good parents I know - wonderful mother I bet

Children come from all around
Each one has a unique background
They are all different and that's okay
Each one living in his or her own way

Children are special in their mother's eyes
Living well or living bad
I wonder whose child

Yes, Who's child
Whose Child could that be
I wonder is it you or is it me

Who's Child

I'll Never Forget

I'll never forget the day daddy left
Yeah, he left us all just sitting there
But momma said it's going to be all right
We're going to make it

I'll never forget when momma went back to school
She said she had to find a way for us to survive
She was so determined and she never quit
I'll never forget

I'll never forget that even when she was tired,
Worked all day and
Went to school at night
She still had time for a laugh and even a hug
I'll never forget

I'll never forget when she said she was sorry
She hit me and left ugly brown and black marks
She said she was so stressed out
She didn't mean to do it - I know she didn't
Because she really loved me
She said I'm sorry and I said I forgive you
I'll never forget

I'll never forget that day I needed a new costume
For the school play
But momma didn't have any money

So she took old curtains and
Thread that she had left from making a quilt
She stitched and stitched even without a pattern
And made the best little costume people could see
Yep - I'll never forget

I'll never forget the time when I didn't get an A on my
    test,
When I was not picked for the cheerleader team
When I was not selected as the best dressed
When I wanted to quit school
But momma said don't give up
You just keep on trying

Yeah she knew what she was talking about
One day I saw my momma walk across that
Stage and get her degree - my biggest hero
She never gave up - she just kept on trying
I'll never forget

I'll never forget momma's ways, momma's love,
Momma's belief in me and momma's belief in herself
And momma's belief in God
Momma is special lady
Because she did it all alone with God's help

I'll never forget

Momma's Kitchen

Pork sausage browned lightly on both sides
The sounds of bacon frying in the iron skillet
Thin crisp and sizzling hot

Hot grits bubbling with cheese
Ready to be dipped on the plate
Scrambled eggs; yellow, light and fluffy
Just enough salt and pepper to bring out the flavor

Soft buttery topped golden biscuits
Ready to be filled with dark, thick, sugar cane syrup
Momma calling.... ya'll wash your hands and
Come to the table
Daddy blessing the food
Hands reaching for the nearest dish
No joking, No laughing, No Sounds except
  Pass me the sausage
  Pass me the eggs
  I want some grits
  You got all the bacon
  Man you greedy
  Hurry up with the biscuits

Then silence

Nothing but the fork hitting the plate and the
Smack of the lips between each bite

Everyone secretly thanking momma for the
Delicious meal as they reach and grab for more!

Momma's Kitchen

Because I Said So

Momma, Can I go to the movies?
No!
Why?
Because I said so!
Momma, Davina said her momma said she can go to the
  game... Can I go?
No!
Why?
Because I said so! That's why!
Momma, Jackie's momma said she can go to the prom
  when she gets fourteen, can I go?
No!
Why?
Because I said so and
Jackie's momma ain't your momma
Momma, can I put the dishes in the dishwasher tonight?
No!
Why?
Because I said so - When I was growing up - I had
To wash clothes with a washboard and wash dishes with
My hands and I didn't ask no questions either.

But momma can I please?
No!
But why?
Because I said so!

Hot Plate, Hot Comb and Hair Grease

Just got through getting my hair washed,
But that's not enough
Momma wants it nice and straight
Same words every Saturday
  Sit down and don't move
  Hold your head down
  Pull your ear back
  Be Still
She would reach for the hot comb
From the hot plate,
I would shrivel and bop my head down

Be still girl and don't move
I think to myself - It's going to burn I just
Know it
Momma it's burning
Girl that's just the hair grease hot on your head

Secretly wishing to get up
Heat from the comb warming my neck
Barely breathing while the smoke rises
As the hot comb comes back and forth from
The hot plate

Never knowing if I'll still have hair when she's finished
Momma slowly pulls the comb through
To press out the thick curly locks

Finally after about what seemed like hours
It's over
Clean, pressed, shiny, straight black hair

Memories

Memories, o' precious memories
Memories of one so loving and kind
Memories of my dear mother

Mother, I know you've long been gone
But I just can't forget all the love you've shown
Mother, I know you left me many, many years ago
But I still hear your laughing voice
I remember the patience you would always show

Mother, I wish you were here with me
I'm in need of your advice
I have a slight problem you see
The doctors say I'll be all right
But I'm scared
Cause I remember your struggle and
I remember your fight

Mother, what would you tell me, what would you say
Something inspiring I know, in your own special way

Your memory is leading me mother
I think I hear your voice out there
You would say kneel down on your knees child
Take it to the Lord in prayer

Yes, mother I really miss you

And all the special things that you would do
I am proud of the way you raised me
I know you would be proud of me too

Memories, o' precious memories
Memories of one so loving and so kind
Memories of my dear mother

Moan and Groan

Wash the dishes
Dry the dishes

Clean the sink
Scrub the commode

Wash the clothes
Fold the clothes
Iron the clothes
Put up the clothes

Dust the tables
Sweep the floor
Mop the floor

C-l-e-a-n
Clean, Clean
Clean, Clean, Clean

I believe that's why mothers have children
Just so they can clean up!

A Child's Plea

Momma will you help me please
I am having a hard time can't you see
I see that man you like, why don't you like me?
God I'm Waiting

I need you momma
Please cook me a meal tonight
You cooked that man a big meal
Even after you had a fight
God I'm Waiting

Momma why don't you put that beer bottle down
It makes me so sad - can't you see my frown
God I'm Waiting

Momma , please help me
Please momma stretch out your hand
I can't take another day of living
In this hate filled sinful land
God I'm Waiting

Momma, Momma why won't you listen
I just don't understand you, please help me God
I know there's something you can do
God I'm Waiting

Momma, please listen to me

I talked to God last night
He told me to keep holding on
He's going to help me win the fight
God I'm Waiting

Momma put down that crack pipe
Return to your old self
That's the person I miss
You even had time to listen and give me a hug and a kiss
God I'm Waiting

Momma, Can't you see I'm heartbroken?
Don't you see my eyes wet?
Can't you feel my hands empty?
Don't you know my ears are open to you?
Can't you see my feet standing still
Waiting for you?
Momma, Momma, Momma -
Please Help me
God I'm Waiting

Pray with me momma - just like you use to
You're the one who taught me to lean on Him
Why don't you?
God I'm Waiting

I know daddy left us momma
But he can't help 'cause he died
You gotta be strong for me momma
I know God is on our side
God I'm Waiting

Yes, thank you Lord
Momma I hear your prayer

Keep on praying momma - God is there
Don't get up yet - it might take God a while
But He's going to answer you
Because you are His child

Thank you Lord for answering my prayer
I always knew that you were there
Momma, I prayed to God that you would change
You just had to believe you could
Because of my faith in God
I always knew that you would

Thank you Lord for hearing my plea
Thank you momma for loving me

Listen to Me - Me

Ain't got no money
Ain't got no time
Ain't gone let chu do dat
Ain't goin' to no sto'
Ain't chu pose to be doin' yo homework
Ain't chu got some money from yo dadde
Ain't chu ole a nuff to cook yo own food

Yeah but,

Ain't chu my momma?

A Letter for You

Dear Mother,

I wrote you a letter last night
To tell you a little bit more about my life
When I was growing up,
I saw you in a lot of heartache and pain,
but you took care of all of us just the same
When I needed your help
You never turned your back
I remember you disciplining me
But sometimes you cut some slack

Now momma, I'm all grown up
And your guidance is leading me now
I'm making my own decision and through
Your motherly kindness
You've shown me how

Something else momma
I just want to say I'm sorry
For all the times I knew I should
But some place deep in my heart
I always knew you understood

My life has been filled
With many ups and downs,
Joy and laughter, tears and frowns

Successes and failures
Whatever was dished to me
You were always by my side
Forever grateful I will be

Thank you momma for all that you did
And all that you still do
I just want to say
I really, really love you

       Love,
       Your Child

Thank You Momma

Somewhere along life's way
People need to take time to say
Thank you momma
A hug, a kiss, a simple smile
Everything you did
You made it all worthwhile
I just want to say - Thank you momma

You gave me guidance and advice
In the toughest of life's situations
You always believed in me
No matter what my decisions
I just want to say - Thank you momma

No matter what the obstacle that was put before me
You always helped me to be the best that I could be
You were my biggest supporter
My biggest fan
You were always there to help me carryout the plan
Thank you momma

God has really blessed me, by you giving me life
You carried me over the years through all my pain and
 strife
A big problem a little problem whatever the case would
 be

You were always there to guide, to mold, and to teach
  me
You gave your time and your energy
To help me see tough times through
Not only did you encourage me to give my best,
But you always gave the best of you
Thank you momma

Thank you for your love
Thank you for your time
Thank you for your nurture
Thank you for your discipline
Thank you for being there
Thank you for your example
I just want to say, I just have to say

Thank you momma!

Journal

Reflections

ABOUT THE AUTHOR

Melvina D. Crawl is a Georgia native and mother of three. She has worked for the past twenty years in the public and private sectors. She is an author, poet, life coach, grant writer, motivational speaker, counselor and consultant.

Melvina enjoys traveling, writing, and helping others. She has excelled in her career and received numerous awards including being named Early Childhood Professional of the Year, Teacher of the Year, Outstanding Facilitator, and Outstanding Citizen Award. She holds several certifications including being a National Certified Counselor.

Her company, Premier Elite Solutions, LLC has expertise in the following areas: health and wellness, personal and professional development.

Melvina's passions are personal development and professional learning. She has written and facilitated many personal development and professional learning courses and workshops during the past fifteen years.

Contact Melvina via her website at www.premiersolutions4u.com, email: info@premiersolutions4u.com, and follow her on social media:

Instagram: premier_elite
Twitter: premier_elite4u
Facebook: facebook/premierelitesolutions/

www.ingramcontent.com/pod-product-compliance
Lightning Source LLC
LaVergne TN
LVHW051200080426
835508LV00021B/2726